Through Jane's Eyes...

Lessons learned from Dr. Jane Goodall

Written and Illustrated by fourth-grade students

at Mendon Center Elementary

in Pittsford, NY

Scholastic Inc.   New York Toronto London Auckland Sydney New Delhi Hong Kong

ORIGINAL COVER

We dedicate this book to Dr. Jane Goodall who has inspired us to make a difference.

INTRODUCTION

Jane Goodall is an inspiration for children around the world. At a young age, many told her "Jane, forget about this nonsense with Africa, dream about things you can achieve."

Those harsh words inspired Jane to bring her dream of making a difference in Africa to reality. Not only did Jane save a species from the brink of extinction, but she continues to empower children by showing them how to carry on her work and make their world a better place.

Jane speaks with her whole heart, and she moved us to write this book in order to spread her message. In the words of Jane, "Children can change the world."

Through Jane's eyes we learned
to never stop asking questions...

As a child, Jane was not only curious, but willing to wait for answers

that inspiration

can come from

unlikely places...

It was stories of Tarzan and Dr. Dolittle that
motivated Jane to travel to
the jungles of Africa to help the animals
in the wild.

and that when you want something bad enough, you work for it.

It was expensive to travel to Africa so Jane worked as a

waitress to save enough money for the trip.

Through Jane's eyes we learned

that dreams have no boundaries...

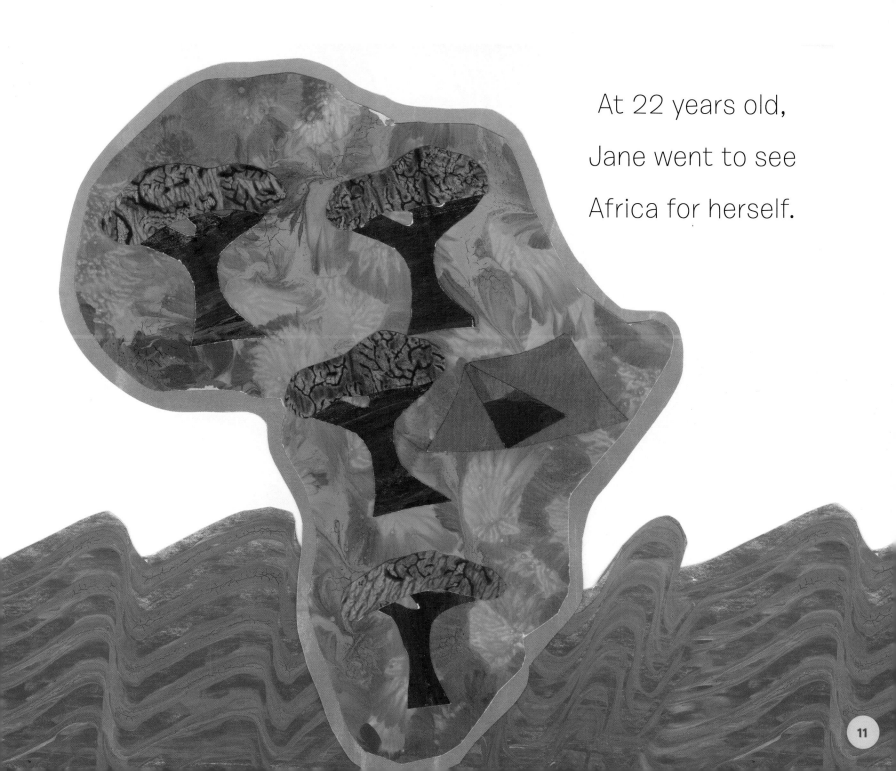

At 22 years old, Jane went to see Africa for herself.

to be grateful for those

who believe in you...

Jane's mother supported her unconditionally,
even when others doubted her.

and that patience has its rewards.

Jane sat for hours observing and learning about the chimpanzees and how they live.

Through Jane's eyes we learned that
trust is not built overnight...

For several months, the chimpanzees
kept their distance from Jane until
one chimpanzee finally accepted
a banana from her.

that things aren't always what they seem...

Jane was surprised to see that chimpanzees could make and use tools in many ways.

and that letting go is
one of life's hardest tasks.

Jane said goodbye to her beloved chimpanzees to share her discoveries and influence with the world.

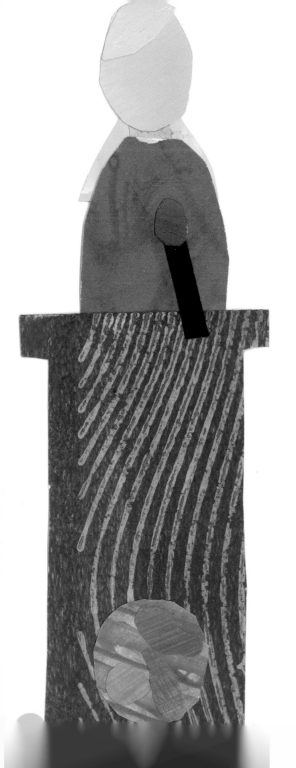

Through Jane's eyes we learned to speak

for those without a voice...

Jane travels 300 days a year to teach the world about ways to conserve and protect animals in their environment.

that everyone

has the potential

to break

barriers...

Jane is a trailblazer who sets an example for women with dreams of becoming researchers and champions for the environment.

and that we need to be empowered to act.

Jane started Roots and Shoots, a program whose mission is to inspire children to make the world a better place for people, animals, and the environment.

Through Jane's eyes we learned that it only takes one person to spread hope to the world.

"You cannot get through a single day without having an impact on the world around you. What you do makes a difference, and you have to decide what kind of difference you want to make."

Dr. Jane Goodall

MEET THE AUTHORS

Front row (left to right): Heather Clayton, Maria Pietropaoli, Lori Lefkowitz, Avery Wilson, Vinay Pendri, Allie Finkbeiner, Careena Sondhi, Addie Froula, Emma Berg, Sophia Albano, Aiwen Li, Adam Gursslin, Alan Raskin, Kim Hosbach

Second Row (left to right): Ethan Hess, Kilian BaileyShea, Alexis Ahle, Anna Guisto, Ally Vicks, Mitchell Green, Lea Mancarella, Andrew McDermott, Lilia Howland, Audrey Hoffend, Jack Garland, Carson Charbonneau, Ashaaz Imroz, Cornelia Crumley

Kids Are Authors®

Books written by children for children

The Kids Are Authors® Competition was established in 1986 to encourage children to read and to become involved in the creative process of writing.

Since then, thousands of children have written and illustrated books as participants in the Kids Are Authors® Competition.

The winning books in the annual competition are published by Scholastic Inc.
and are distributed by Scholastic Book Fairs throughout the United States.

For more information:

Kids Are Authors® 1080 Greenwood Blvd.; Lake Mary, FL 32746 or visit our web site at: www.scholastic.com/kidsareauthors

ISBN 13: 978-0-545-92473-3   12 11 10 9 8 7 6 5 4 3 2 1

Cover design by Bill Henderson

Printed and bound in the U.S.A.   First Printing, June 2015

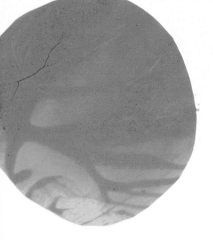